PRAISE FOR STACY DYSON

Stacy Ardis Dyson's name should go along with the statement 'precision in performance'. She is the master of coordinating a spoken word performance to perfectly balance storytelling and emotive impact. Her plethora of work lionizes the human reality within culture and provides real world experience to life's complexity.

— *GENEVIEVE RAY, author of FREE ROAMING ADULT WOMAN*

Stacy Dyson is the kind of poet who sneaks into the deepest levels of your being with her words. Her narratives have the ability to dismantle myths and plant knowledge. Her poems are portals to understanding.

— *SUSANA PRAVER-PEREZ, author of RETURN AGAINST THE FLOW (Juan Felipe Herrera Best Poetry Book Award) and HURRICANES, LOVE AFFAIRS, AND OTHER DISASTERS*

Stacy Dyson is a master of storytelling and capturing audiences. Her work has a way of resonating with people of all backgrounds. Her lived experiences and knowledge makes her a staple voice in modern Spoken Word spaces and shelves across the world. If ever the word Griot was a perfect title, it would encompass the fire that is Stacy Dyson!!!

— *SHOCKIE G, author of IN LIEU OF FLOWERS and EXIT WOUNDS: Bullets and Butterflies*

The writing of Miss Stacy Dyson puts me in a place of presence. There's nowhere else I need to be when I'm reading or hearing her words. With themes ranging from revolutionary to romantic, from heart-wrenching to hilarious, the pieces of her poetry puzzle provide me soulful enrichment with every return. And I'm always ready for one more.

— *NATE ABAURREA, author of the*
BACKROADS AND BORDERLINES trilogy

Stacy Ardis Dyson is a matriarch of resistance poetry. Her voice speaks truth thunder that makes foundations of power quake. And just when you're about to burn the whole damn house of cards down, she finds a heartstring or two to tug on. Stand ready for a full array of the feels.

— *BEAR WOLFE, Poet*

A true master of storytelling, Stacy Dyson doesn't just recite poetry—she pulls you into an experience. Every word feels intentional, every pause carries weight, and the imagery she creates lingers long after the poem ends. An incredible talent who has the rare ability to captivate an audience from the very first line.

— *BLACK NOISE, author of I CRY OVER SPILLED INK*

Stacy Dyson's poetry has the power to move, to rattle, to shake, to open the door onto resonating possibilities. Her lyrical narratives make me think, ponder, feel. She shared with me a poem about a mother, not her mother, not my mother, who had been lynched in a tree, a tree that her granddaughter, blissfully unknowingly, loved, and I felt the pain and the compassion, the weight of history and the burden of responsibility. For that mother, ultimately, is my mother, her mother, our mother. This is a collection of poetry that should be read and cherished.

— *JOSEPHINE LoRe, author of IN MY FATHER'S HOUSE and THE MOON AND ALL HER FACES*

Stacy Ardis Dyson is a voice for the Divine Feminine, not only the side of the feminine that nurtures and holds, but the side that also wildly fights for justice, for reckoning, for restoration. Her poetry is palpable, her imagery pulses on the page, reading like hymns sung to soothe and protect the suffering, hymns that function both as prayer and incantation. In a world that's on fire by the crimes of a failing patriarchy, Dyson's work reminds us how the feminine energy will salvage the suffering through community. Through poets and curators like Stacy Ardis Dyson, who create poems for women in the trenches, poems about a better world that's possible.

— *K.R. MORRISON, poet, educator, moon witch, author of CAULDRONS*

What do you reveal to yourself when you tumble headlong into Stacy Dyson's poetry, or happen to witness her reading her own work?

You stumble joyfully upon yourself— seen. Lyrically cradled and nurtured. When Stacy speaks (up) boldly for herself in every instance, she is in full awareness that, as she lifts herself up in her writing, she carries *undaunted spirit* upon her capable shoulders— her forebearers, her sisters, known and yet to be met, a precariously-tiered, threatening-to-topple goodness still existing (but by a wispy thread) in humanity.

She bears this weight of knowledge in her words with grace. She proclaims all our lives, lived fully, when she declares her own truth.

> — *PHYNNE~BELLE, Editor, Mayari Literature,*
> *Co-Editor, PGNP, Organizer, Phynnecabulary Presents*

Stacy Dyson is a poet who is unafraid to tackle issues of race, oppression, gender and social injustice with unflinching honesty, She employs emotions that are fierce, loving, sad and empathic. Her work unapologetically celebrates her identity and black femaleness. Her vision calls out for self-love. She challenges us to consider our role as humans in a world that continues to systematically oppress our fellow human beings. She calls out to us to rise above structures of oppression with courage and compassion.

Her powerful message is urgently needed. We need more poets like Stacy Dyson.

> — *KEITH MAR, Poet*

An Artist, A Truth Sayer, A Singer, A Sister, A Warrior. Profoundly personal, Ms. Dyson's work will hit you with a gut punch, cloak you with truths and school you in the trials and tribulations of navigating everyday life. Deeply painful yet full of joy, fierce yet passionate, the breadth and depth of her work invites the reader to fathom the complexities of Black culture; racial identity, spirituality, isolation, relationships and womanhood. Soulful and honest, she shines a light on uncharted shadows, every purposeful word is palpable, leaving you with nowhere to hide. BECAUSE THE SUN WOULD NOT MOVE is a must for every bookshelf.

— *JANE SPOKENWORD, Poet, Spoken Word Performer, Speaker, Visual Artist, Workshop Facilitator*

I always thought it was trite when they said that when the student is ready, the teacher appears. What can I say? Stacy and I met by happenstance and, as a writer honing my voice, from the outset it was immediately apparent that Stacy will be an important teacher on my journey. Stacy's poignant and practical insights are always drawn from her personal experiences and journeys. Each session with Stacy has always been a koan... while the sessions helped me move forward each week, the lessons continue to linger and build on each other even all these months later. When I read Stacy's poetry and am moved by her words, I also recognize the multiple layers of meaning from the subtle to the accessible. I've had many writing teachers over the years, and somehow I know I have done something to please the gods to have been gifted time with Stacy Dyson.

— *DEEPA MEHTA, Writer*

BECAUSE THE SUN WOULD NOT MOVE

STACY DYSON

Red Thread Publishing LLC. 2026

Write to **info@redthreadbooks.com** if you are interested in publishing with Red Thread Publishing. Learn more about publications or foreign rights acquisitions of our catalog of books: www.redthreadbooks.com

Ebook ISBN: 979-8-89294-046-7

Paperback ISBN: 979-8-89294-045-0

Hardcover ISBN: 979-8-89294-047-4

Cover Art: Kimberly KMA Anderson

Cover Design: Red Thread Designs

CONTENTS

FOREWORD

I've always identified as a nomad; even when I was a little girl, I dreamed about traveling from place to place.... learning, exploring, doing my poetry. It was all I wanted. I never felt settled in one place, didn't even want that. I wanted to, needed to be in motion. And singing. Always singing.

Riding high in Colorado, career on blast, love life on flow, traveling to perform or teach..it was great. I used to joke that I only went home to visit my clothes. There was one year I remember when I packed my suitcase in first week of April and never truly unpacked til end of October. I loved coming home to my apartment, but too many days there, and I would start fretting, anxious for the next trip. Yes, I was tired... a LOT. But deliriously happy.

Then I got sick, lost my love, and (shortly thereafter) my apartment. My sister had been urging me to San Diego, so I sold up, packed up, and moved. Said I'd give myself six months to like it or leave. Fell head over heels in love with the place after two weeks.

As much as I loved California, the first few years were rough. A fight with my sister ended with me moving from space to space, paying for the privilege of discomfort and/or inconvenience. But, at least I always managed to have a roof...sometimes for weeks, sometimes months.

And in the meantime, my professional life stayed on trajectory...lectures, coaching, performances...not enough to get a place of my own, but enough to stay moving, stay motivated. I was homeless, for all intents, but never landed in a shelter or on the street. I did everything I could to make sure I didn't have to go back to Colorado. That would have been a step back in so many ways, and I needed to stay in moving forward.

I was born to be nomad; moving has never bothered me. And while a lot of those moves (and there were a LOT) weren't all that comfortable, I made the best of the situation, kept working. That saved me...as long as I could practice my craft, as long as I could keep writing/performing/teaching, I was okay.

Thought once I'd finally found a place to settle. Establish a home base. I lived in perfect contentment for 5 years at the bottom of a friend's garden. My own space, work moving forward, two books written, students...I still performed out of town, but at the end of those shows I had a place of my own to go back to. Then, completely out of nowhere, I was asked to leave. Had to dust off my traveling shoes and get gone. I originally settled on Texas, but there were things happening there that made me too uncomfortable. I started having nightmares about my nephews coming from Odessa to drive me down. So, I settled on New Mexico. It's been a year; I'm in a lovely space. I'm trying to feel safe, but I can never go to sleep without a contingency plan in mind. Health and the world have made the prospect of moving AGAIN a very real possibility. A move wouldn't make me happy, but I would make it through. Not at all gracefully, but through.

Because here's the thing: I figured out long ago that no matter the storms...personal or professional..I had to stay in motion. I couldn't /can't take the risk of my words, my ideas dying from being tethered or getting stale. The world stays the same in that people live and die, loves wax and wane. Good and evil take turns winning out. The globe keeps spinning. Stars still dance about in night skies. The sun does not move.

And no matter what, my words and heart need to stay free. I have to be able to hear other people sing their songs, as well as continue to sing my own. So, if another move (or, God forbid, moves) become my reality, I'll take it as meant...another step in the nomad's journey. I might not be comfortable or happy, but I'll be telling my truth and staying in motion.

Because the sun will not move.

But I have to.

1

PLEASE, NO

Do not let the aliens come disguised as Black women

'cause if TV is all they've studied, then they be draggin' fake nail, fake hair and loud "Yass Queen" interruptions in normal or polite conversations

or just loud and ignorant for no good reason

(if we need to be that, we always have a good reason)

They will say they've studied history and x-rays

so they know what

we are composed of

but you can't x-ray pain

or burden

there is not enough history to tell

the truth of how we're daily betrayed by a country we help build/still maintain

and are tasked with saving on the regular

Don't let them come in as Black women

they won't know where the fingersnaps

go

right

where the laughing and heartache go

right

where the laughs fit right

where the burden of learning

to be

to know

to take care of

go

right

Let them come back as something innocuous

or innocent

(we are neither of those)

let them come back non-threatening and unprepared

(we are neither of those)

Let them come ready to marvel /and wanna be/and fear

(not just a little)

the only folks on the planet who *truly* understand

what surviving on this planet

really means.

2

YOU BEST TO KNOW HER NAME
(FOR JENNIFER)

Her name is Marissa Alexander

make sure you put some respect on that name

folk still debating over whether she had the right

to participate in her own survival

she hit the ceiling because the bullet

wasn't meant to hit him

she hit the ceiling because she had to hit back and she couldn't take
the chance

of laying hands

guns aren't the only actions that backfire

her name is Darnella Frazier

you need to put some respect on that name

she filmed the murder heard 'round the world

and folks wondered why she didn't drop her camera

and do something

a little Black girl in this jacked-up world

what was she supposed to do?

get herself hurt or killed

trying to fight back?

or do what she did

and bear witness in the best way she could

Her name is Fani Willis

you best lay some respect

on her name

The death threats come every day now

the big stupid bad is making it his business

to question every breath she takes

and his followers are balanced on the edge of his lies

ready to take aim

The law is supposed to convict him

and protect her

She is going to prosecute, she is going to make sure

liars and thieves and people who persist in trying to steal

the last vestiges of the american dream

pay the toll

She has been cajoled, warned, threatened

"Back off before you get dead"

What is she supposed to do?

Abandon her promises?

Black women don't do that

and we only run when there is no other way

because we know

you have to be alive to fight

Faith and the marshals are watching her now

but all that prayer won't stop a bullet

Her name is Simone Biles

best lay some respect on that name

Reigning queen of the stratosphere

nobody could toy with air and movement the way she did

til one day she stopped

her light-trippin' needed to rest

before she hurt herself

So she laid down a minute

And the world jeered and called her soft

questioned her commitment

talked smack about how some people get spoiled and

can't take the heat

What was she supposed to do?

Keep risking injury to define the true nature of light and its movement

risk injury so people could keep making money

off the way she could bend time between dance steps, grit,

and moves that showed the old routines the door and told them not to come back?

Die so y'all could keep bragging that she was our free pass to show the world what Black folk can do, how America is always the excellent?

how dare she think of herself

how *dare* she?

Folks tend to forget

a star always knows how to spin in the heavens

But the star doesn't

She didn't

Somewhere along the way

y'all need to lose that attitude

Black women get to self-love /self-care

protect themselves

and you don't have to like it

approve or co-sign on our

life decisions

Keep your second-guessing and insults to yourself

we're grown and we know how to act

the world better be grateful for the fact

that we pay such close attention

and let us be, let us breathe

how we're intended to.

3

SONG
(FOR SIERRA)

Darlin', you're right

I do think you're fine

crazy sexy, intelligent, cool and sugar-sweet

a gentleman, a scholar

I imagine in your wake lie a thousand satiated hearts and satisfied bodies

I am not that kind of girl

you gonna have to step to me different

because loving me

is a revolutionary act

I should not need to, but

I'll save you some time

let me tell you

exactly who I am

I am the girl who stuffs music into her ears because the glittering burn of words tumbling along the strands and threads of my DNA often leaves no room for other sounds

Truth is an old faithful lover

Integrity is my bff

you can't live with them always hangin' out

you best get steppin' now

I feel no need to

but let me tell you

exactly

who I am

I am the girl who breathes in flame, then breathes out poetry and falling stars

never met a fantasy I could not completely enslave

to kiss me is to discover how the light in a sapphire

tastes

to know how it feels to catch errant stars laughing between your fingers

To kiss me is celebrate every woman who ever loved

never mind if it was at a loss

she loved

and made herself a part of history

To love me you must bring everything

your wit /your sword /your sense /your shield/ your strength

be prepared to overthrow old patterns and awkward understanding

tired conventions and over -familiar acknowledgements of

what commitment should be

I don't need a dragonslayer

I got that shit

I need a dreams-keeper

A man to handle my body can be found

with any quick look and careless smile

Can you handle my visions as well as my bad dreams?

I don't need you to understand me

I understand me

I don't need you to complete or save me

too late for that

My parents loved me enough to make me whole

and Jesus saved me when I was 12

Are you getting this?

You're going to have to wrap your head around

your heart around

your life around

the fact that I am not that kind of girl

the ones you're used to beguiling and

being beguiled by

Bring your honor and your A-game, Sugar

and let's go warrior together

change some worlds

with our sharply defined, luscious "all that" and

unique /ambitious/realized selves

Yeah, Sug

you should probably stretch first

breathe deep

'Cause once I let you in

be in for the long haul

I am not another sweet/ pleasant pastime

I am not capable of

impossible to be

just another comfortably satisfied heart

and gratefully satiated body

Because loving me

loving

me

is a revolutionary act.

4

I CAN'T (STAY)

My hands, mainly

I cannot get the smell of bleach away from my nostrils

it's resident on my clothes

the house clings to it, it mixes with last meals and

the last of my comfort for a while

But mainly it's on my hands

Cleaning/scrubbing

incessant/unceasing

uncaring

it only wants to make things clean

It doesn't care what this move is costing me

it doesn't mind that I am wiping counters and scrubbing floors

with thoughts and feelings acrid as any corroding fume

I wouldn't mind so much

but even my lavender soap

can't get the smell off my hands

and I begin to worry

I have been worried

that there is some chemical composition bound together by tears

and betrayal

that makes a scent too angry, too hungry

to forget to exist

clings itself to every fingertip

I smell it in my sleep

Eating

walking through newly empty rooms

I smell it in my sleep

on my hands

the lavender will not wash it away

I cannot wash it away

the pain and regret and

very real anger I am feeling right now

salt water, bleach, pain

What does that combine into?

Is it the chemical composition for despair?

For grief?

For some mutt amalgam of everything I am feeling right now?

I want to smell flowers and yeast bread and the soup I simmered last
night

a smile in my throat, my words

and hope

I want to smell, I need to smell a least a mist of hope

What is the chemistry, the composition of this loss, what does it
make,

this heartbreaking?

my heart breaking

Because all I can smell

is bleach.

5

I COULDN'T (GO)

Well, I'm not moving to Texas any more

I know it's all I've talked about for months

don't get me wrong, I was seriously thrilled

when my friend gifted me an RV

I had to move, didn't want to fly

because you know, COVID

and people being generally nasty

and me being non -trusting and suspicious of folk's personal hygiene

Anyway

I was thrilled

had called my nephews who live in Odessa

"Your auntie is coming down.

Why don't y'all come get me, we can make up for some lost time

Lost years."

It was the paperwork holding us up

the tags and plates came, it all started to be real

and then it was just waiting for the title

I did the research, everybody said "Well yeah

you can drive without it

as long as it's recorded somewhere"

And I had the receipt, I knew that electronically it was on file, it existed

but I needed it in my hand

I had to have that small square piece of paper in my hand

Because I had two young Black men coming to drive me

into Texas

and I could not/did not feel sure or safe

without that little small piece of paper in my hands

There was some hold up, some glitch

it kept getting delayed

And I was starting to get eaten up with this dread, this fear

taking over all of my chest

when I said "Oh yes, my nephews are going to drive me there"

My two young Black nephews were going to drive me there

I sounded brave

but I would put down the phone or get off the chat and my hands would shake

I could feel the quaver in my voice, I kept having to wipe tears off my face and clothes

because my two young Black nephews were coming to drive me

into Texas

in an RV with shiny new plates and tags recently gifted me

Legalities and civil rights never seem to make a difference down there

unless it's on the side of the police or old vindictive white men or laws that should have been off the books decades ago

should have never existed

and I had two young Black men driving a newly titled RV and their aunt who is old enough to remember girls being blown up in Sunday school and why "Strange Fruit" is still a necessary, bitter reminder, sung in mother's tears and defiant desperation, and folks who have died whilst engaged in the unholy commission of BEING WHILE BLACK

The delay was longer than expected

that's when I started having the nightmares

my boys

(yes, they're grown, but they will always be my boys)

breezing through a dust-blue Texas night

stars showering down the way they do in the panhandle sometime

laughing, listening to their Grand-Dad's favorite Motown and Silk Sonic

then the cop blows out of nowhere

Steps off his bike, puts his hand on his holster

because these are two young Black men in a newly gifted RV and it's a long, lonely highway and he is bored or

maybe they passed a stop sign a little too soon

or maybe he hasn't made his quota for the night

or maybe just because they are two young Black men laughing and not caring where they are

except to come get me where I wanted to go

He wants the paperwork, license, registration

he sees the name on the papers isn't theirs

tells them to step out

they're smart, they've been trained the way we have to train our children these days with the police

They step, they are quiet, they do not talk back, give attitude

but I know my boys

and their eyes are angry and their mouths and throats are tight

and they are swallowing humiliation and remembering the story I told them about their Grand-Dad being pulled over with me in the car

and that title

that title is shaking in their hands along with the license and registration

and the cop takes their angry eyes and tight mouths as a threat

at least that is what he will say in court

that he "feared for his life"

and they will face down on the lonely highway, maybe still alive

maybe not

I should have been happy, but I got sick when it came

I felt as if I would be handing them a death warrant

and I could not let a piece of paper kill my boys

could not let some small square piece of paper be the thing

that let some cop murder my two young Black men

under a Texas sky

I've been a lot of things to my guys

I would not be the messenger of the thing

that might get them killed

And I know you're saying that's ridiculous, or that they could be stopped anywhere

but right now, Texas is a place where murdered children's cries are still echoing in school corridors

where the destiny of a woman's freedom to her body is not a recognized fact

where there are still sun-down towns and a need for The New Green Book

and two young Black men singing Motown and Silk Sonic under a star-rushed sky is an invitation to death

I couldn't do it

I can't do it

Don't get me wrong, I am so grateful for the gift

the RV can be rented out or lived in if times get tougher

I still haven't touched the title or the envelope it came in

it hurts to touch it

it feels a little too heavy in my hand

I will fly to see my boys

and the only thing in my hands will be their favorite cookies

and heartfelt invitation to come see me

The nightmares have stopped

my boys are still in Odessa

and me

well

I'm not moving to Texas anymore.

6

EVAN
(YOU COULD HAVE BEEN BRAVE)

I send you music because I cannot touch you

(yet)

I'm good, but I'm not that good

my lips cannot reach yours across a continent

my tongue cannot explore every inch of that

ooh- baby -make -me -ache body from however many miles away

but I can send the music

send a seduction

message a massage

it serves to bank a fire

that cannot be extinguished

Again, Sugar, don't get me wrong

I'm very,

very

good

but not that good

I cannot dampen an ardor that has grown

from the moment I heard my language

leave your mouth

that poet's tongue beguiles me

touches me when you cannot

where you haven't

(Yet. But you will. Of that, I have no doubt)

I send you music because

watching your body move for 24 hours

would be too exhausting

and too exciting

and ultimately

not satisfying enough

for my hunger

Because the sound that interests

intoxicates us

is my way of saying

"Any

time

you have

time

we can keep

time"

Until I'm free to catch your rhythm between my hands

I search archives for songs that make my throat and heart and body

ache

mostly for you

the ache is overdue and pleasurable

I don't want it to go away

You are overdue and pleasurable

I don't want you to go away

(I hope I've made that clear)

I send you music

because I can't summon you like a wish

but for now, I have to treat you like one

Charming One

you disturb me in all the right ways

please

keep moving

to the music I send you

fingers and smile and

soon,

I can stop wearing my fingers on my

laptop keys

and

let them dance all and over

your beautiful,

beckoning

light.

7

MOVES/ALL THE GROOVES

I could dance, I just couldn't speak the language

mi companera, Jessie, said

"Mija, you don't need to worry.

Those hips will tell everybody whatever you need to say.

Let them speak for you"

So when Rhythm noticed me and began to flower compliments in Spanish

he just smiled when I said

"I'm sorry, I can't understand"

He kissed my hand and smiled

"Don't worry, Baby

You already told me "Thank you"

When you began to dance."

Rhythm became my last heartbeat

he made me sing

Rhythm made me shout

Rhythm made me come

to the realization of belief

to the certainty

I had only ever flirted with before

That my body and spirit and soul knew

what I needed to say

had said it already

I just needed to let my fingers record the testimony

So when Rhythm died

whispering Spanish love songs in my ears

his heart melted into my bloodstream

his sweet-breathed compliments fell into my footstep

and took me back to the church

and the salsa palace

the lilt and sway of the songs is the same

I don't believe the Lord differentiates

as long as the words are sung in faith

And Rythm never minds which way I move

He just kisses the hands of my soul

and tells me to dance

I already know what I need to say.

8

GRATITUDE

I measured it once

4 paces to the couch that is my bed for the last year

12 steps to a bathroom shared with two young children, their mother, one vain/out of control teenager and a boarder who lurches through the hall (7 paces) most nights drunk or high and incapable of zeroing in on the toilet bowl

I am supposed to be grateful, I am supposed to thank my lucky stars

I am supposed to bite my tongue til it bleeds when

I clean what stays dirtier

I cook and it's wasted

I can't ask for quiet because it's not my house

I am a guest, I should be grateful

the dirty, constant chaos

I haven't been as sick in 5 years as I've been in one year here the air is dirt and dust, the children bring germs

nothing is ever clean for longer than an hour

I'm never safe to shower til I bleach everything first

It is all noise and dirt and air that is making me sick

But I am a guest

I am supposed to be grateful

This country lied to me

told me it would serve, protect

praise my merit, sing my songs

and all the while

maintain my sense of pride in this place

Turns out

I am simply a guest that is supposed to be grateful

nothing stays clean for a day, an hour

rough and terrible times banner the news

what feels like every 5 minutes

I fought, I did

I fight, I do

but nothing stays clean

it just gets dirtier

and I can't sleep

the noise of losing all my rights

and most of my freedom will not

let me sleep

This land was never meant for me

and that is a hard thing to learn

a harder thing to know

almost impossible to live with

I cannot bite my tongue til it bleeds

but I do have to break my heart that way

til it bleeds

the noise and filth in the air

is making me sick

I bleach everything

shower in hot, hot water scented of waterlilies

but the stench of government breaks through it all

the stink of being lied to all my life

breaks through it all

I measured it once

every breathing space

the space shrinks and screams and

is smaller with every move I make

every move we make

but this is for our good

They say

this will save us

save this country

They say

They cheat, they lie, they rape

our souls, our minds, hearts

and steal our gratitude

by any means necessary

because we are Black

and Brown

and women here

simply guests who should work and suffer and shut up

if the pain is more than we were promised

This place is not ours, it never was

I doubt it will ever be

I have been lied to all my life, it seems

and my daring to howl in protest

is frowned on, beaten down, relegated to my "place"

this is not our country

we are being told, our contributions mean nothing, our lives mean less

you see, we are Black and Brown and women here

we are only servants and trouble and problems

we are only guests here

And we are supposed to be grateful.

9

SUPLICA A LOS VIENTOS

Mi padre named me Rosa

he said it was so I would always be reminded

of pretty things

flowers and light and love

That is very hard to do

in this border camp

where everything is despair and lost hope

harsh light and broken families

yo no soy una flor, yo soy una nina

If I were a flower

I could ride in the band of my father's hat

the only one he ever owned

the brim was cracked, with ragged edge

but the headband was strong

tempered with sun and sweat from the labors

that made the money to bring us across

I wonder if he still has the hat

or if somebody took it away from him, threw it away

they way they took his daughter

and threw her away

When I was young, I remember

my mami bending in to kiss my papi welcome home

I stood between, one hand wrapped around my mother's knee

one around my father's

a rose

growing strong and vibrant in the fragrance of their love for each other

I cannot feel that sun now

just the lights that shine constantly overhead

If I was a flower

I would be in his pocket, fragrant and close to his heartbeat

close to where he kept the money to make the coyotes

not look at me and say

evil things, lick their lips and say

evil things

I don't have much English

but I know what they said was wrong

made my father hold my hand tighter than he ever did when we walked at home

hold me closer/ shielding me when they passed by to count

how many souls they planned to release to the desert or deserted alleyways or dark, cold stretches of strange highways

Not look at me like the guard here

looks at me

that guard, he looks at me

the way I remember the bad, drunken men looking at the

bodies of the women on the street

the soldiers looking at the bodies of women on the street

he looks at me

that way

The older women they tell me stay away from him

pull me into chores or conversation when he is near

try and hide me away from his glances

but when he sees me in the halls or my room or on the playing field he watches me

he looks at me like the soldiers, like the drunks and bad men

watched the bodies of women in the street

Once, he ran his hand over my hair and smiled and said

"Que linda chica

You're a pretty thing, aren't you?"

The older women surrounded me, pulled me away

but they cannot always be close and I am afraid

because sometimes he comes for the older girls

and they come back very quiet and very sad

and I can feel their fear

sometimes they cry out when they sleep

They run and pull me away, too

lie down by my bed, but they do not sleep then

their eyes are open to watch for me

to protect me

But they cannot stay awake forever

Papi, he used to take me to count the stars

watch the cool earth with the moon, singing

singing to me so that I would learn not to be afraid of the night

I am always afraid now

Roses stand strong against the wind, call the rain sister.

breathe free air

yo no soy una flor

I am a little girl

mi madre es muerta

mi padre is out in the world

without me

One day, una mariposa landed on the windows

a rose can talk to a butterfly

Right?

I asked her to please find my father

so he can take me to where I find rest, breathe free air

feel the night sing gentle with the moon

Sometimes I do not think I have another season

I may never see mi papi again

the butterfly may never deliver my message

Why should she?

Butterflies only talk to flowers

and I am not a flower

I am just a little girl

Yo no soy una flor

I am not a flower

yo soy una nina

I am just a little girl.

I am just a little girl.

10

QUERY ('CAUSE SOMEBODY HAS TO KNOW)

So, airport coming out of Tennessee

sharp banging noises, somebody yelled "GUNFIRE!"

and the place shut down

flights cancelled, runway closed

TSA line stretched all the way to the back of the building

And the only people on the floor

Black and Brown women

soothing, explaining

the only people on the floor

Black and Brown women

taking care, solving problems

Black and Brown women making sure that everyone is taken care of and okay

My show got zoom-bombed in August

filthy racist screaming

filthy pornographic images

so, I killed the cameras

apologized to the guest

put up a closed session

and did the show

Another day soothing and explaining

another day taking care/solving problems

another day being

a strong Black woman

I had nightmares all week

Sick stomach, headaches

and nobody knew except for the one sister I had to call

because I had work to do and couldn't fall apart

I had work to do and needed to protect my people

I had work to do

and strong Black women take care/soothe/ protect/ solve problems

Right?

Kamala Harris took over the nomination

people started breathing again

got hope again

felt like maybe we weren't going to die

through errant Trump-idity

Gets called bitch

she smiles

gets called half-breed

she walks light and hopeful

Gets the entire weight of the free world

dumped at her feet and is required to smile and laugh and be strong
and protect and care

solve problems/ be a strong Black woman

doing what strong Black women do

and lookin' good while we do it

Another sister on the floor holding hearts together

'cause that's the job

Right?

That's what we're born and bred to do

Right?

stay calm, keep it together

teach/ soothe/hold up /hold out /hold it in

til you can get somewhere private

and even then

don't take too long

because somebody needs feeding or holding or help

Knowing that

knowing that to be true

knowing that

knowing that there is nothing to be gained in telling you

that blinding/ painful truth

come closer, let me ask you something

When do I get to lose my shit?

Our mothers bade us stand straight

so that we did not dirty our wings in the dust

our fathers bade us stand up

so that our crowns did not roll into the gutter

but the world

the world

bled us, beat us, stole our children

made us responsible for holding up

the damned sky all the damned time

then said

"Oh, by the way

We need just a little more

Sister

You got just a little more in ya

Don't cha, Sister?"

The least protected and most abused

the lowest paid whilst bulk of the workforce

the ones who create the movements

then get buried in the dust of the rush

to correctly frame the story

The world envies and imitates

craves our lips /our hips/ the way we style our hair

our joy/our dancing

but when they are looking for ways to deny/ to denigrate

to bring down

they come for us

How we fix our hair—Simone Biles

how we sing our laugh-Kamala Harris

how we fix our mouths to say whatever we need to say

Me

and every other sister who keeps telling the truth

And then we are loud and extra and manly and wrong

until the world comes running to us

Again

to make it all right

I would like

for just a day

to be valued

I would like

for just a day

to have my contributions recognized

past what I do for other people

I would like

just for one

got-damned day

to not hear the word "resilient"

used to describe me

that's not a description

it's a dismissal and death warrant

all rolled into one

I would like for my sisters to stop believing and being told

that our worth depends on what we do and who we are

for our people

I want Black men to stop using us as an icon or an excuse

I want white women to stop using us as a crutch or repository or a vessel to constantly drink from but never replenish

I want white men to stop thinking of us as an exotic trophy, a revenge on their ancestors

an aggravating source of the children that crowd your welfare rolls, ruin your schools, and raise your property taxes

and that day is gonna come

believe me

But not right

not right now

not next year, not in the next twenty years

because there is too much at stake

and the world hasn't learned to hold itself together yet

We can't jump ship because

believe me

we'll get everybody else on the lifeboats and get left to drown

'Cause that's the job

Right?

soothe, comfort, and protect everybody else first

And I want to stand on this mic and howl

I want to stand on this mic and cuss/ scream /

shake the whole earth with stories about where my heart

and all the bodies are buried

but I can't

because I have little sisters coming up under me

whose way will be blocked/ banned /buried

if I tell all the truth at this moment in time

So alright, not tonight

or tomorrow

or...

I don't know when

But I need to ask

America /Africa

every island/ every continent

anywhere there is a sister

holdin' it down/ holding on/

crying in the dark

or having to hold herself so tight

that her heart doesn't have room to break

My frustration, my life

needs a calm, a clear

not defined by what other people need /demand from me

Seriously, World

I am a Black woman trying to live through the burn of reality

in this world

and I gotta know

When do I get to lose my shit?

11

IN HONOR OF SONYA MASSEY

The tears don't help you do the work

they blur the screen, leave you trying to scrub wet salt and horror

off your hands

recreate, re-invent the memory of every other pain you've

tried to write away

Your voice gets hoarse

your instrument becomes your torment

because you can't cry, it strangles the syllables

You can't breathe shallow

you need the air in your passages

to tell the truth

And anyway, what good does it do?

Your sisters still get shot for going about

their lives for no good reason

going about their lives

I am tired of writing poems mourning Black women who were just minding their own damned business.

You read the reports and your eyes begin to burn and there is no use

in crying

Crying doesn't stop bullets

crying doesn't stop insanity

crying doesn't stop the threat of being murdered for

playing games with children

smoking a cigarette

boiling water

sleeping

But you have to know

you have to read the reports and watch the videos

and suffer

You have to feel like the weight of a thousand years

is never going to be off your shoulders

because their names need to be said

at least once

in celebration of their lives

just once

in celebration

of their lives

Not as martyr or icon or

the reason for a revolution

Just spoken as

person

as people

as women just trying to make a way

make it through

Live

as person

Live

without the threat of becoming the

focus of a movement

But your eyes burn

and you rebuke yourself

run to your pen, try and make it right

the only way you know how

try to make it right the only way left to you

Try to not tremble while you write the piece

sing the piece

your eyes are burning

but you can't cry

Don't cry

(not where anyone can see you)

Remind yourself

this has happened before

you know the drill, why are you surprised?

Remind yourself

this has happened before

You can't

you can't give up

you can't give up the right, the right to be surprised

and hurt

and desperate

(so hurt, so exhausted

so desperate)

Because someone has to sing all their song

someone has to mix the pain/anger/salt-sweat streaming /utter betrayal

produced by this country

into ink that breeds firestorms

Because the tears

(alone)

the tears don't help you

do the work.

12

FOR GEN

Sometimes, Honey.

sometimes, it just needs a sistah

someone whose DNA is drenched in your personal history

who doesn't necessarily

love what you love

but understands the reasons for your affection

someone whose hand can hold (and be held)

from a lights -year away

'Cause sometimes

sometimes Life goes out of its way

to try and break you

whether with dreams or memories

or the cacophony of coulda/shoulda/maybe I would have

if I had been more capable/more brave/

less deviled by the demons in my pocket

The bad tears feast on those times

years/days/ hours apart

it doesn't matter

(it never matters)

'Cause, Honey, those tears lie in wait

Oh, the traps are clever

it might be a word or look

one lyric, one seemingly innocent inconvenience or life note

meandering by, looking harmless

a thing that brought you joy or sorrowed you

something could at least have the decency to be ignored

til it was convenient for you to deal with it

SNAP!

the trap springs

and your whole body becomes the playing-field

for *those* tears

for *that* pain

and teardrops become rivers

and rivers become something to drown you

It's a hard way to go down, Honey

that's when you need a sistah

who understands your mind

carries your heartbeat in/into

her existence

who will set fire to her clock, talk smoke to her calendar

tell her lover to go play

'cause grown folk talkin'

who will set (temporary) fire to other obligations (if need be)

just to make sure you're warm

She is what keeps you

in check/on game/

clothed in the best version of your possibilities

However

she cannot be perfect

she will not be fragile

she is required to have tempers and bad days

times where she dropkicks her crown, crushes it in the dirt

then watches it roll into the closest gutter

She is required to know

that you carry her heartbeat into your existence

She will find it necessary to be on

the most intimate terms

with all kinds of crying and every joyful possibility

existing in the same body

in her body

She will have no doubt

that fires are set

from the light of the way you love her

will understand that nothing more than

or less will do

This is God's gift for daring to be a woman in this world

and living in the best way to tell your tale

She will come unbidden

and always just in time

to save your life

over and still and again

This is the Lord saying

"No, I did not send you out here alone

I knew how it would be

to be yourself, to push the cost of what it is

to be yourself

to leave you ultimately singing in the

narrow places of your life

And the wider spaces of your everpresent."

"I will give you two things" said God

Hope

and her.

'Cause sometimes, Honey

it's just gonna need a sistah."

13

POET 12-STEP

I have long maintained most open mics resemble an AA meeting

which thought was confirmed the night I saw in the chat

"Thank you for your share"

and that's when I knew any line between the two was artificial

So please bow your heads for our prayer:

God grant me the serenity to not put a contract out on pretenders who are wasting my time

The courage to acknowledge spirit- singers that the rest of the audience may not snap fingers for

And the wisdom to know the difference

Before we get started, a few housekeeping notes:

coffee and cookies in the back

please make sure the space is clean for the next group

parking out front is free til 10

and

don't even worry about admitting you have a problem

You're a poet.

Need we say more?

Step 1

Be humble and mean it

The Lord did not single you out, She just picked you special. Get your head around that.

Step 2

Sincerity or originality. Nothing else will do. If you borrow, bend the knee to their name. If somebody borrows/ copies/ quotes you wrong without your consent, track them down. Put a curse on their bones, then call tell their mama and tell her it was you. That's right, scorch their earth and leave nothing behind.

We'll wait.

Step 3

Quit kissing on that mic like it's an old flame you trying to convince that it really was that good and they know you have to come back for more. You wanna put your mouth on something so bad, drink every syllable and its intent deep into your soul, then lay your lips accordingly.

Step back and respect the sensation. I promise you, do it like you're meant, and the intent will kiss you (and the audience) right back.

Step 4

The pain is not going away. Deal with it. Remember the worst day of your life. Dip your pen deep and write til blood runs from the tip. Don't stop until the pain is manageable. Because the pain is not going away.

Step 5

Wrap your head around the most profound joy you've ever felt. Dip your pen deep and write til golden –bright thought sparks, gratitude that breathes in flame and laughter, and a sensation that you are all that and the absolute shit runs from the tip of your pen. Don't stop, just swallow and smile. Deal with it. The joy is not going away.

Daily Affirmation:

Damn straight this is a real job. That's right, I said it. So there.

Step 6

This it is most definitely not all about you. Really. It isn't. Stop thinking so.

We'll wait.

Step 7

Get down on your knees and beg your ancestors' pardon for not calling their names and saying "thank you" after flowing a piece that you know calls fire down from the sky. There are no amends you can make. Just don't be stupid and do it again, 'cause neither your grandma or mine is having it.

Daily Affirmation:

I will tell my truth today. I will open my soul to the truth today. I will not hide from that truth no matter how not sweet/less comforting /non-pretty is shows itself to be. And if I fail in any of this, I will shut my mouth til I remember who I am and what I was born to do.

Step 8

Get your nose out your notes, hold your head up, and act like some-body raised you right. We don't care about your forehead, so quit showing it to us. Stand or sit straight, look us in the eye, and stop mumble -talking. Stop leaning on your nerves or first times or "this is new." Enunciate your glory/your homage/ your knowledge/the stories you are blessed to sing. And if I have to tell you again, we can call up your ancestors, your mama, and any possible descendants (**see Step 7**) and have them explain real sacrifice to you.

Step 9

Comes in three sections:

Part 1

Do not explain your piece.

Part 2

Do not explain your piece.

Part 3

Please expect curled lip, pure ennui, and an enduring lack of interest if you explain your piece.

Don't. (and no, I am not saying please)

Step 10

Rinse, repeat, and remember Step 9. I'm not saying I'm gonna hurt you if you forget. But somebody will.

Step 11

This is still not about you. Believe me.

Daily Affirmation

Know that the world is waiting for you to help them breathe, cry, or sing. Dream in that belief. Sleep in it. Then get on that stage, breathe deep, and let the people know.

They matter. You care.

They needs be heard. You can messenger their heart.

You can and must and will clarify how it is to live/survive/bleed/dance in this place, in their space.

Step 12

The Lord blessed you. Your ancestors /parents/ partners taught you.

This is a sacred charge. Treat it that way.

And do your damned job. Do **our** damned job.

Open your mouth, breathe deep, look clear.

And do your dammed job.

14

SAY YOUR PIECE RIGHT

Not every poem is your evil old grandma who's whipping your butt with a 20-year-old wooden spoon that she inherited from *her* grandma or a fresh peach-tree branch she made you go cut

or that bully boy from down the street who pulled your hair, stole your lunch and homework

and lied about you wetting the bed

Know sometimes the poem is to be caressed like the lover who ran his lips and hands over your hips and thigh

breathing slow to slow time

because 5,034 hours of living/loving you

was never going to be enough

or a baby learning to soothe itself asleep to the waterfall mist that sings in your lullabies

Learn how your poem is to be reverenced

(yes, the piece is to be reverenced)

but sometimes worship comes in the form of tough love or calling out

So get street with your poem, call the dozens on it

make it afraid you're gonna have to come off your job to go to the school and conference with its teacher

You can't sing every song the same

stop trying, stop lying about what needs to be said

excusing it by saying

"It doesn't fit the form "or "I just wrote this" or "it's not finished"

Let the craft speak to you the way

your soul speaks to the wind

whatever song evolves

is needed by your entire body

(or somebody you might never know)

it doesn't matter

You're not writing for yourself, you're writing for the truth

you are not the important one here

your comfort is not the object of the game

Let it hurt, let it go

do it honor, do it joy

do it so your granma doesn't have to come out her final laying-down place

and cut that peach -tree switch

Love it enough to wave "God bless"

step up on that stage

step up on that mic

breathe clear

And say your piece.

RIGHT.

15

TALK TO THE SHIELD

Wrote my first play at university

I had been a poet since I was five and in kindergarten

but I needed something new, something more

a vocal extension

I had seen Ntozake Shange dissect/ illuminate

the lives of Black women

I knew I didn't have her fire-song

but I based the play on what I'd seen /what I knew

what I was learning

Those words stole every moment of my life

sat in class writing notes on the characters

waked head down 'cross the campus

hearing dialogues in my head

The excitement, the exhilaration of working

in that world

writing five women in conversation, in revelation, in tears

while we forced laughter out of our lives

(you know, the way we do sometimes)

I can't describe

it was my whole life

I remember when I was working on the very last pages

Roy, my then boyfriend, came over

to take me dancing

leaned over to kiss me

Almost killed him snarling "I'M WORKING"!

never even looked up

it was a couple of hours til he spoke to me again

(we never did go dancing, though)

Then I pitched the play to the

Black Student Alliance

I needed a producer and knew

they would do it proud

waited longer than I should have thought

til the president agreed to meet with me

he was late

I remember that

he swaggered up, made a few complimentary comments

then said "It would be better if you had a man in there,

people would like it better,

more people would come"

I said no

He told me they wouldn't produce it

without a man being a

big part of the play

swaggered away, left me sitting, angry

proud he'd had the last word

Oh, the play got put on

I took it to the university council

they picked it right up

and when the BSA saw how much

publicity it was getting

they

begged

to be listed as the co-sponsor

to save embarrassment

When I created DragonsWing

I pulled women together to create a presence, create a voice

in the world

I was surrounded by military bases

and military men

who hinted or outright bold said

"It can't be just women

You need men in there,

people will like it better,

they'll listen more."

We did just fine

If poetry was in the air in that city

it meant Dragonswing women were

breathing life into the moment

into the movement

til I wore myself out, got sick

and had to leave

had to let that dream breathe without me

Doing a two -woman show

my character was righteously angry

direct enough to create painful fires

and walk through them dressed in

what was real

came out burned (but resolute)

on the other side

We only did one show

but two days after

the woman who had shared stage with me

came and said

"My friend, Joel, you made him uncomfortable,

he asked if you had a man right now,

said it might calm you down

give you something worthwhile to focus on."

I have a million stories like that

any woman who walks through the world

empowering (or trying to)

other women

can sit and

tell those tales til kingdom come

I swear, it never stops

It never goes away

Last spring in Silver City

Ridin' high, glowing after

talking about my life and my firesingers,

women of wit and inspiration

women who will someday run this sorry world

and elevate to its true potential

I heard "Well, there ought to be men in there"

It was supposed to be sotto voce

I heard it clear as a bell

from a man who had admired /applauded my mission

just an hour before

If I had charged him with it

asked for an explanation

offered discussion

he would have denied it

or defended it

I let him sulk and stew about it

I couldn't be/can't be bothered to care

I have/we have

been called selfish, elitist

exclusionary

told I surround myself with women

because I can't get a man

That I do this because I'm not enough to keep a husband and get children

told time and over again

I need a man to make it right

to make it legit

to make it acceptable or get it blessed

because "We deserve to get our voices heard, too."

I never denied that

But what I know is y'all have opportunities, can make ways I can't

get to spaces where a woman making a demand

for her voice to be included

is laughed down, talked down

Told "Men only.

Ours be the important voices.

Y'all can come pick up the scraps when we get through,

Be good, maybe we'll leave you something."

I have seen women pushed to the end of lists

back of the stage

shut down, being told

"We had a choice between you and a man,

the audience will like him better,

his words will be more seen, respected,

listened to."

Been lectured on how to sing my words

walk onto the stage

how to dress so the audience will play more attention

And when I pushed (push) back

I'm branded difficult or ball-busting or

mad

'cause I

(again)

don't have a husband or get children

I am never seen as righteously angry

just spoiled or manhating or too damned smart and strong

for my own good

I know after this poem

I will get comments and complaints

I will hear, "We're not like that,

I'm not like that."

I will hear what you deserve

how I should accommodate your voice

in what I'm building right now

Someone (most likely someman)

is bound to bring up

why I don't have a husband, haven't gotten children

how I must hate men then

I'll get some angry looks, cat or whisper-called

"Bitch"

might pick up some threats on the way to my ride

(yes, that's happened too)

I do not defend

I will not explain

because real warriors never indulge in fighting each other

they simply get on with the battle

So

Talk to the shield, Fellahs

Talk to the shield.

16

YEAH, GOT PLAYED (ALL OF US)

In '64 I was told

"In school

be good, get smart

obey the rules

Move your people ahead

be a guiding light

and it will be different, you wait and see

It will be different

Wait

Do your best

and wait"

my parents had both

lived deep in jim crow

change came crooked, change came slow

colored bathrooms and fountains

bodies burnt black in trees

yes, my people had joy

but never had ease

"Stay in church, stay in school.

Be the difference" they heard

And my parents and theirs

believed those words

and they made sure their girls

Paid heed and heard

how it would be different

"Do the work and see

Just persevere, and you'll see"

My daddy was army

And young and Black

fought for a land that did not

love him back

fought so our people

could stop the fight

for fair and just and

legal and right

so his daughters and grandsons would never be

scared to live every way but free

"It will be different"

He promised me

"It will be different

Just wait, you'll see"

I waited, did what I was

raised to do

shined a light, followed law

marched and sang and changed

the world any way I could

been 60-some years

watching my people rise and fall and

taste of joy

show pride

but I have had to remember the whole time

not to believe, not to wait for ease

I used to fight, get indignant

when folks swore

ease would never come

and for the last ten years

all I can feel and taste

in winds that should be blowing freedom

is defeat singed with lies

I feel like a fool for believing

It would ever be different

You see

you see

I was not raised to accept defeat

as a comfortable settled

established sweet

but hood-wearing cross burners

sit government seats

put migrants on airplanes

Tagged, sold,and stamped

to what we know are concentration camps

our courts are for sale

and white dollars win

if you're not rich and white

you pay for their sins

And I still burn with

will to fight

but I know what's true

and this world is not right

Or just or fair or balanced or free

I wake every morning

with my father's voice in my ears

my ancestors echoing their desires /yearnings

for just a breath

and I struggle, I do

but it hurts to know I've been lied to my entire life

that my time on this planet has been

surrounded by breach of trust

laws so fragile that 6 paid -for voices

can erase it with a pen stroke and no conscience

Keep fighting yeah

Keep singing yeah

as I say in one of my other poems

"I have no choice because I have a voice"

Change will come

I'll be long time dead

change has to come

but I'll never see it

Things will get different

'cause they have to be

But I'll be long underground

Before we get free.

17

FOR KING JACKAL

Why people still believe that one foot in what the world calls correct

(or lets you get away with)

gives you leave to be

rude (at best)

wrong (at worst and altogether)

especially when the other foot is ready to slip

(probably already slipping)

into the grave of "It's okay for me to be filth

because I'm better than you

or your life

or your circumstances.

God won't look at your petty self

the way He looks at me"

is mystifying and

anger-making

Just so you know ('cause all those cowards around you think it, but won't say,

too busy trying to grease themselves up enough to pass through the eye of a needle

too busy trying to rinse the taste of hourly murder out of their mouths)

Let me tell you

I will take the word of every 'ho on every corner, every hustler in the game, every non-apologetic soul

who tells the truth about who they are and what/why

they do

who breathes the truth whether it is

sweet or not

dressed up pretty or educated

gentle-said

painful or not

over anything you say for all my days

and beyond

To not understand why (or say that you don't)

is only the first of the many thousand stinging, insulting lies for which you will answer to my Lord

good luck with that.

18

THEY'LL ASK WHY

The house, my grandma said

the house has to smell a certain way

bathrooms of lavender and bleach

front room linen-fresh air and roses

lady's bedroom lilac water and talcum

and the kitchen

the kitchen needs to smell of love

and hard work

sweet tea and the cornbread mix for supper

baked ham on Sundays

ginger /nutmeg /pumpkin spice

for to mark the holidays

I loved Granny's house

it was warm and smelled good

we'd sit on the burnt -white front porch

after laundry- times or baking days

talking this and that

singing sometime

The tree

cottonwood or some such

whispering with wind-secrets and birdsong

cool and Lord knows how old

leafy- green and branches for swinging or

climbing or sometime a good cut-me switch

if Granny caught you mouthin' wrong or acting out

One laundry morning

Granny and me on the porch

listening to the breeze make soft and sweet games with the flowers around

Granny sat quiet, eyes far away

I thought she was resting or fixing to start telling me

the best way for biscuits to rise or how to fold and place a sachet

but she just kept quiet, eyes far away

and when I got impatient, commencing to dabble my toes in the air scheming on asking for lemonade

or some such, I don't remember

Granny sat quiet, eyes fixed further away than I had ever seen

I didn't know the voice she finally said in

had never heard that much pain or anger in her throat

never heard her tears pent up and soaking every bone

til they turned hard as marble couldn't be moved or lifted

Granny said.

"I hate that tree,

hated it all my life.

But I'll never cut it down,

I can't ever cut it down.

My mama, your great -grand

my mama

she tended us, tended house

did some launderin' for white folks in town

She was quiet, mostly

warn't a fancy, doll -pretty woman

but people fancied her smile, her ways

She was real smart, too

taught us all stars and singing and

some books, and the Bible

loved to hear her children laugh and read

Mama came home one day

warn't smiling, just quiet,

seemed to draw a long, determined breath

then sat here, right where I am now

and told me

told me like chains were wrapped around her heart

and pulling her down into dead

She said

"I slapped Mas' Johnson in the street today.

He had his hands on Saide from the grocery,

twisting, bending her arms just to make her hurt,

no good reason, just to make his friends laugh.

And when he saw me watching,

he threw her down, spit like she was cheap gin

or some kinda dirt

not even good enough to farm in.

I watched him come for me, let him get close

I could have run, didn't feel to

just stood there

And when he reached for me

I slapped him, hard

like when I'm cleaning the parlor rugs.

Hard and loud, it left a mark

I saw it rise blood-red against that burnt ghost-white skin.

I could have run or begged or

cried or something.

maybe should have

But I just stood there, not shaking, not swaying fit to faint

It was all quiet, him and his no -count friends were all quiet,

Saide was laid loud-sobbing in the dirt

I got her to her feet, told her I'd mend her dress,

told her to take a bath in some of that rose-scent water I'd brought last week.

Mas' Johnson, he just stood and watched me

all quiet, him and his no-count burnt-ghost friends

Then he said "Well,

we'll be by your place tonight."

Guess I was supposed to cry or beg or somethin'

run or somethin'

I couldn't, didn't feel to

I just said, "I got laundry on the line."

turned my back and walked home."

My granma said

"When your great -grand came home,

she sat for a minute

staring far off, just quiet

then raised up, saying

"I got laundry on the line."

Set a hard broom to the parlor and hallways

made her bed and sacheted the bureau drawers

scrubbed the bathrooms bleach and sunshine clean

then baked and roasted

stirred and boiled and poured

lemonade, Sunday ham, drop biscuits, molasses cake

the big stewpot full of greens, celery -onion potato salad

And when every room smelled exactly right

when the house smelt proper as it should

she bid us all to Aunt Julie's

told us to hasten and hold hands

said she'd send for Saide to fetch us

said not to tarry, to make sure we

weren't around and evident when it got dark

Used a voice I'd never heard before

like rusted iron and dagger-glass

was running in her veins

Turns out they hung my mama

from that tree

came late when the wind was playing up

came late when a cold moon was splitting the thick branches

set her body up high, left her burnt-black and twisted

hung her knowing no account would be required

'cause she was just some nigra woman

didn't know her place

Law took no real notice of such things back then

Hung her and rode off

hooting and laughing, most likely

thinking themselves brave and fearless

or some such

knowing they had

upheld the code, revenged their honor

or some such

Your great-grand, they laid her out nice

her best dress and a fancy hat

folks sang real pretty at the church,

ate food in the hard-broomed front parlor, went home

life went on, the story passed down

I went off to work and school

house came down to me."

Granny stood, looked at me straight

like rust iron and broken diamond ran in her veins

"You'll do the same as me,

go off to work and school.

House will come to you.

Make sure you keep it proper."

I live here now

I hard -broom the front parlor and hallways

make sure the bathrooms smell of bleach and lavender

my bedroom fragrances of violets and talcum powder

And the kitchen,

the kitchen smells of love and hard work

sweet tea and the cornbread mix for supper

Baked ham on Sundays

ginger /nutmeg/ pumpkin spice

for to call the holidays

The tree

the tree a cottonwood or some-such,

whispering with wind secrets and bird music

cool and Lord knows how old

leaf- green and branches for climbing

or sometime a good cut -me switch

sometimes late, the wind plays up

sometimes late, an ice -cold moon splits the thick, crooked, fired-black branches

I hate that tree

since my grandma told

but I won't cut it down

I hate that tree

forever

but I will never cut it down.

I can't ever cut it down.

19

THE SCIENCE OF SAID
(FOR DAKISHA)

For the job on Academy

I had to call in twice the week before

to conference with the office manager

she was nice, we got business done

laughed about some things

I didn't step in the office til the next Monday

she was polite, but confused

thought I was in the wrong place

because quite honestly, Black folks were not seen that

far up Academy Boulevard in those days

Like I say, she was polite

but confused

apologized, said she was waiting for the new receptionist

and when I said "I'm her,

I'm Stacy"

before she could stop herself

the words came flying

"You can't be. I spoke to Stacy twice,

she's..."

(yeah, knew what she thought I was)

Now, sometimes I'll let that go

(sometimes we all let that go)

Sometimes I'm feeling playful or evil or just inclined to make folks

finish (well, defend) the thought

I'd had to get up early, hardcurl my hair

put on pantyhose, switch buses three times

and still walk in looking cool, calm and creased sharp enough to cut glass

I was not feeling generous

So I half-smiled and let her swing

"What I meant was...

I mean, I spoke to Stacy twice and...

I just expected..."

She finally gathered her wits, stopped sputtering

and said "You just look so... young,

you sounded so much older on the phone"

I just gave her the rest of my half -smile

and went to work

she was nice enough, but the relief when I finished the week

was dense enough to touch

There is home talk

and how to speak in public

if you are Black or of color

you know what I'm saying

because the world can be cruel, is judgmental

parents, grandmas, aunties, all the elders

bred (sometimes beat) into you

the way your mouth better hold syllables

depending on where you were

With some folks, it was to show off

some folks, it was meant for education

some just loved the way of high- flown sounds

in the mouth, in the ear, on the wind

but for all of us

Black or of color

it is protection

That is the essence of code-switching

it's not just about fitting in where you are

it's about saving time, saving embarrassment

saving your life

and like any skill, it is designed to save your soul

or your skin

a little bit

There have been whole chapters written

speeches given, studies done

but no one talks about how it hurts

how exhausting it is

how anger-making

It's like any other chameleon exercise

meant to make you safe enough

to get to where you can be

alone or free

or safe

In San Francisco

healing up from a broken heart

the city decided to welcome me

with an earthquake

it wasn't bad, I'd been jostled harder on the stairs during school- day

fire drills

Listening to the radio after, the DJ asked to call in if it was

"your first time"

was crackin' on all the out-of-towners freaking over a few points

on the Richter scale

I called in, laughed with him some, talked about how it made me

kind of nervous to walk down the hill to the Italian bakery for a
fudge cake

but how, sometimes, you overcome for the important things

He said "it's cool you reached out,

we don't get many white folks calling the station"

I said "I'm not, what made you think that?"

It got real quiet for pretty long

the radio went to commercial

He came back on the phone, said

"I'm sorry, you just spoke...

I mean, you sounded...'

I didn't say a word

was kinda insulted my own folks didn't know me

kinda resigned to it, too

After a minute, he said "Thanks again for calling in,

what's your favorite song?"

He played it when he went live again

after the commercial

See, being double -tongued can work against you, too

I have been made fun of, threatened

for not sounding Black enough

been told I'm trying to show off or act like I'm better

"Get your nose out of the air, Girl

you're no better than me.

You better remember you're Black."

I never forget

believe me

I also never forget how much those times

leave deep-scored pain marks on my spirit

believe me

Because you don't stop to analyze how they might feel

indignant or inadequate or can't take what really shouldn't be a surprise

You just remember being laughed at or called out

or told how you can't be Black sounding like that

talking like that

You play between Scylla and Charybdis

you can be their version of "down" all hours

or heed the voice of your parents/ your aunties/ your elders

on what your voice is supposed to do

Okay, last example

courtroom hallway

had just finished testimony against Kelly

some crazed chick

had abandoned her baby for a crack house

then claimed kidnapping when two friends and me

took Meghan Siobahn to her granna three states over

Granna's lawyer went on and on

about my testimony, how it was flawless,

guaranteed to make the judge rule Grandma Laura's way

He pumped my hand up and down

smiled deep in my eyes, and said

'Where did you go to school?"

"University of Northern Colorado.

Why?"

"Because I'm always telling the street kids I work with

that if they just learned to speak properly, it would make such a difference."

I stopped smiling, took my hand away

he was too busy congratulating himself to notice

I've regretted not answering that back for 30 years

I swallowed hard, then

I'd shake his world and make him hurt

now

I was polite then

I am not

now

I should have told him

should have lashed him into silence

with the truth

that I learned to speak that way at home

university added a little disdain

not polish or vocabulary

my parents had me trained

before I got anywhere near

UNC's door

Aunties and elders and my parents

taught me how to speak to save my life

years before I got to be insulted by white-boy lawyers

who automatically translated "Black" into "ignorant"

years before I got teased by my Black choir-mates

for using phrases I learned in books

instead of words from dozens on the playground

Do I code switch?

Of course

you cannot be Black or of color in this place

and not do what it takes to fit in, save face

save your life

My parents and aunties and elders taught me how my mouth

better hold syllables

the world taught me how not to expect anything but condescending praise or derision

for being double -tongued

I pay the price in short- lived amusements or victories that taste sweet for a minute

or pain that leaves scars on my spirit for a minute or a few years or my life

All I have ever really wanted

was the right to sing my voice, my words, into the wind

make them land like burning silk or a heat- seeking light

to burn or bind wounds

All I'll ever want

is to be called as "she who sings as she is"

and let it rest

There.

20

GRITS 'N' HONEY

When Daddy told us the grits thing, I was still in school

15, 16 just getting interested in relationships

not sex, just how it worked between men and women

the psychology, sociology of

how folks got together, got along

Let me start by saying

I was a very protected girl

not in the sense of being hovered over

or not encouraged to adventure

I had sisters who would fuss with me

but fight my battles, come push to shove

my mother taught me defense via sharp tongue and wicked wit

the way Southern women do

and my father ...

Well, Daddy was a combat- veteran -golden -gloves -champ

who had a miniature gun collection

and made no secret

that even looking cross-eyed at a girl of his

was not an option

When Daddy told us the grits thing

it was after growing -up years of

watching how my parents danced late in the living room

spent walks holding hands and making mutual, respectful decisions

watching arguments that didn't always end like fairytales

but ended

watching valentines addressed to "his special angel"

watching the pride on her face when he sang with the God's Messengers

Years of watching how men and women needed to relate to each other

years of hearing stories from friends and seeing stuff in other people's houses

that would later make my parents

purse lips or shake disapproving heads, saying

"Nawww" or "We don't do like that"

years of friends whose fathers treated their mothers like property

or stupid or not as good as

talked trash about women with their wives or girls or daughters

looking embarrassed or scared or too beat down to breathe

saying to my father "Bet you wish you had some boys instead of all them girls"

Daddy was never what you might call amused by those words

made sure we didn't spend much time around such folk

made sure we knew better than to listen to men like that

made sure we knew better than to be women like that

When Daddy told us the grits thing

my mother was big into Al Green

y'all know, the soul singer, Arkansas boy

Mr. Let's Stay Together

(which Tina Turner re-did and did better

but I digress)

Women used to swoon, listen tight and late at night

to his sound, my mother got this look of ecstasy and anticipation dancing around the living room

I, personally, had no use for him

too much music too full of himself

besides, I was Stevie's girl (but again, I digress)

Don't know if y'all know

but the true stories of Black entertainment lives

came quick down the Black church and community pipeline

doings and rumors and goings -on were well –known

wayyyy before they hit the "real" news

In '74, Mr. Here I Am Come and Take Me

got stupid with his girl

who paid him back with boiling grits yanked right off the stove

and poured all over his sorry self

and if you were Black, you knew all about it

long before the entertainment mags and papers did

Baptism comes hard some days

ol' Al got religion, became the Reverend Green

right quick in in '76

A little while after, my sisters and me

doing afternoon chores or homework

or something

Daddy called us into the formal dining room

had us sit and be quiet

Asked had we heard about it

"Yeah, we heard."

"Okay.

You know you don't let some man

put his hands on you, right?"

We'd been taught right, we nodded our heads and said

"Well yeah we know,

Daddy. We know".

My father cleared his throat...

(Now, when Daddy cleared his throat

it was about to get deep)

Daddy grunted, cleared his throat, looked us

straight

in our eyes, and said

"Any man ever puts his hands on you

Any man EVER puts his hands on you...

You put some grits on the stove

and call your Daddy.

Y'all got it?"

We got it

That was 40 –some years ago

my Daddy's been gone 15 years and more

there have been a fair number of fellahs

some just out for sex

some exploring relationships

I've watched and listened and learned

I'm better at understanding the psychology,

the sociology

of how folks get and

stay together

I remember being taught right

by years of fights that didn't always end in fairytales

pride in each other and valentines

I am forever open to the psychology, the sociology, of men and
women

and how we get together,

I deeply believe in equal decisions dancing late at night in the living -
room

That being said

every kitchen I've ever lived in

features several large pots for boiling

And at least one

freshly purchased

box of grits.

21

VOW
(THANKS TO RAYJANE)

Being who I am is a 24/7

no breaks, no days off

what I was born to be, born to do in this world

has always been apparent

no apologies, no questions

And on the days and nights where I toss or cry because

I hurt or I'm past overtired or I really just cannot take it still/again/one more

damned time

You

are there

Pushing, scolding, lecturing, singing

Comforting, singing

pulling me

Singing

you are always there

And I

I need to remember

I have to remember why I'm here

how I got this place

the debt

to my before -borns

to my grandparents (whether I met you or not)

to my father, my mother

even in my darkest times

I have not forgotten you

I owe you

and I'm good for it, I promise

Days are

times are turning very dark around here

right now

I could let my heart break, but I can't find /can't take time to

clean up the mess

there is too much left for me to do

I suppose I could step back

but I don't know how

I suppose I could run away

I don't know how

I wish I could fold my wings and live quiet and keep still and

just let my words dance for me alone

make pretty wall-pictures in my mind

but you hobbled my soul with grace and responsibility

you chained my heart to passion and possible

you made sure that I would never escape the confines of

Honor

I don't know how

because

I have not forgotten you

I owe you

and I'm good for it, I promise

Sometimes that promise

is all that will let me breathe

most days, that promise

is my personal life- saver

keeps me from drowning in seas of trouble or treason

(or my own exhausted tears)

Hell, with what the world is bringing my way

I will need that promise to act as heartbeat

til my heart stops liable to break

You always said I was hard -headed

but you also said I never forgot a word you said

and I haven't

I don't

I wouldn't dare

Because every tear, every joy

every pain, every exultation

is for you

and the ones before me

and the ones coming up

I might not sing loud

but I'm keeping on singing

might not breathe easy

but I'm in and ex -haling clear

the walk forward mightn't be steady

but I move

(I'm gonna always move)

It is flow -written on my heart

tempered in my bones

I was born swaddled in affirmation

baptized in belief

and anybody who knows me

knows this girl keeps her promises

doesn't matter what it costs

So y'all can lay your heads down

rest light

Your girl has not got lost

My head is kept up

My back is kept straight

you can sleep

knowing

I have not forgotten you

I owe you

And I'm good for it

I promise.

ACKNOWLEDGMENTS

Writing this book has been incredibly difficult. And honestly, there were times I wasn't at all sure I'd make it through. So many people (especially my sistergirls) held my hand, talked me up (or down), kept me in prayer...the loves of my life made this book not only possible, but necessary.

This book is for:

My fellahs. Curt, Justice, Alic...Y'all remind me so much of your Grand-Dad, it hurts, sometimes. Love y'all to the moon and back, forever.

My grand-niece, Taliah. Bright, brilliant, accomplished...beautiful on every level, inside and out. You are pure Dyson Girl. No more needs be said. I love you past all sense and reason.

The fire-singers of TESORO. My hopes and dreams embodied. Ladies, you are brilliant. Each and every one of you. Never to mention the *craziest* crew I've been part of in a WHILE. May your voices dance forever in the wind. Mucho mucho amor, chicas.

Renay. You've helped me keep breathing in more ways than one. All love, Sis.

Bridget. whom I have not (hopefully) driven completely mad in the last year, and whom I daily bless for not having to explain my ...oh, let's call it unconventional...life. I do believe we'll be hanging' out for a minute, Kiddo. Je t'aime.

and, as always

For my Jamaican One. Every other heartbeat still sings for you.

ABOUT THE AUTHOR

Stacy Dyson is a poet, acapella vocalist, playwright specializing in the life and times of the Black woman. "Someone has to sing for my sisters. Their lives, loves, philosophy...I'm lucky enough to be one able to make those voices heard."

She has done program design, residencies, workshops, and live performance all over the United States, and dozens of shows virtually. Author of 7 poetry collections, plus five CDs of poetry and spoken word, she is former Poet Laureate for Imagination Celebration (Colorado Springs) a nominee for Poet Laureate for the State of Colorado, Founder/Lead Poet of DragonsWing (Colorado Springs), CoFounder/Lead Poet for Page to Stage: Womens Words (San Diego), a Colorado Women's Playwriting Festival winner for her play

FANNIE'S GIRLS: A 4-1-1 IN 5- PART ATTITUDE, and a TEDx speaker.

Her last two poetry collections, LOVELY AND SUFFERING and FOLLOW ME ON THIS, focus on her life as a Black woman during the pandemic, and her ten years living in San Diego.

A Literary Titan Book Award winner, she is preparing to launch a women's writing/performance workshop series called FIRESCRIBE. She plans to tour with her newest collection BECAUSE THE SUN WOULD NOT MOVE, while continuing to build her international women's poetry network TESORO "one firesinger at a time."

Connect with Stacy:

poetswind@hotmail.com

www.saintwinterraines.com

RED THREAD BOOKS
—— write - publish - impact ——

About the Publisher

Red Thread Publishing is an award-winning indie press dedicated to amplifying powerful, authentic nonfiction voices. In our first five years, we've published more than 72 books, supported over 400 authors from 30 countries, and celebrated 50 book awards, proof of the impact and quality behind every title we produce.

Our passionate team is committed to guiding authors through every step of the writing and publishing journey so their stories not only get published but make a lasting impact.

Visit **www.redthreadbooks.com**
Email us **info@redthreadbooks.com**

instagram.com/redthreadbooks
facebook.com/redthreadpublishing

www.ingramcontent.com/pod-product-compliance
Lightning Source LLC
Chambersburg PA
CBHW020357130626
46549CB00006B/2321